EVOLUTION

EVOLUTION
AND THE HIGH SCHOOL STUDENT

compiled and edited by Kenneth N. Taylor

Tyndale House Publishers
Wheaton, Illinois

The monkey has become a symbol of evolution, but not properly so. No evolutionist now believes that man evolved from monkeys. The current view is that both man and monkey evolved from the same primate ancestor. The purpose of this book is to find out whether the view is provable, probable, or even possible.

Sixth printing, November 1972

ISBN No. 8423-0800-8

Credits: pp. 5, 71, Tom Schmerler; pp. 9, 14, 23, 54, H. Armstrong Roberts; pp. 12, 49, Radio Times Hulton Picture Library; pp. 16, 33, Harold M. Lambert Studios; p. 18, William Roberts; p. 25, Department of Geology — Wheaton College; p. 31, Gerhard Heilmann; pp. 36, 61, 63, American Museum of Natural History; pp. 41, 50, United Press International; pp. 44, 46, Carol Hilk; p. 47, New York Times

Why all the hangup about evolution?

Why the outcry against it by many Christian parents, and the outcry of many scientists against anyone who doesn't believe it?

What difference does it make whether life "just happened" and then slowly evolved into man, or whether God—a real, personal, all-powerful and all-intelligent God—made everything there is: not "man from monkey" but man and monkey as special creatures from the hand of God, in just about their present shape and form?

Well, there are two main reasons for the controversy.

First, the Christian is ticked off by the strong assertion of some evolutionists that the "fact of evolution" has freed them from "superstition" about the existence of God. So the Christian, with his strong belief in God, naturally wants to believe in something else than evolution if atheism goes along with it.

Second, there is the question of the reliability of the Bible. For the Bible, on which the Christian student rests his faith for both this life and the life to come, seems to teach the instant creation of the man Adam in the Garden of Eden. So if it didn't happen that way, then is the Bible trustworthy? And if not trustworthy in regard to this pre-history, how can it be the Word of God? If the Bible is not true about creation, then what parts of Scripture are true, and how can one decide which are true and which are not?

The purpose of this booklet is to discuss evolution from the viewpoint of the creationist—the person who believes that God created Adam as a full-grown man. The book will show why evolution remains merely a theory, rather than being a fact on which a case against the Bible can be built. Then it will show why the theory does not seem to the creationist to be true, probable, or even possible—despite the fact that almost all biology teachers and textbooks teach it (so we have a lot of explaining to do!).

8   First of all, though, it should be pointed out that disproving evolution or proving creation (or God) is impossible, for there is no solid biological evidence for evolution, and it is difficult to disprove what can't be proved. There are facts, such as human fossils perhaps a million years old. But there are two ways to interpret the facts—the evolutionary interpretation and the creationist interpretation. And neither can claim that the facts prove one position or the other. How could they? For facts that happened apparently millions of years ago are hard to check. About all that can be stated with certainty is that the evolutionist thinks his interpretation of the facts is good, and the creationist thinks his is better.

In other words, one's interpretation depends on one's presuppositions. If one's presupposition is that God created without evolution, then a creationist system is the inevitable result, and all problems resulting from that viewpoint are cleared away by various suggested solutions. And if one assumes that all things emerged in evolution, then the very difficult problems stemming from that point of view are similarly cleared away by the evolutionist as best he can.

Now presuppositions aren't necessarily bad! All of us believe many things we can't *prove,* and this can frequently lead to truth. The creationist, too, has presuppositions: for example, the assumption that there is a God. And we think we have good evidence—answered prayer, changed lives, the universe all around us, fulfilled prophecy, etc. But these are not scientific proofs in the usual sense of the word; and when science ignores or attempts to "disprove" God, we still believe in Him, for He is our presupposition.

Similarly, the evolutionist bases his theory on presuppositions. But in his case the situation is less reasonable, for he is dealing with a scientific theory and he should be able to marshal adequate scientific facts to support his theory. As this paper will try to show, he does not do this, but he nevertheless insists on holding to evolution as an established fact. Instead, he should frankly state that much of the evidence is lacking and that his belief is based primarily on presuppositions; and of course, some do.

So the argument can't be won on the basis of the facts. Neither the evolutionist nor the creationist comes to his conclusion from evidence acceptable under the usual laws of scientific proof. So there is considerable difference here between weight of opinion and weight of evidence!

Charles Darwin (1809-1882).

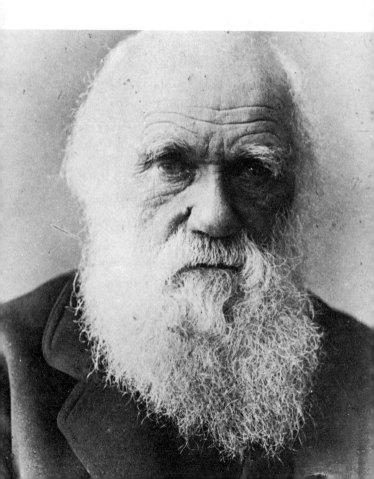

A Bit of History

Now for a bit of history before getting into the arguments pro and con. About a hundred years ago, Charles Darwin began realizing that there are variations in animals of the same kind. Notice, as an example of this, the different races of people, and different kinds of dogs ranging in size from Pekinese to Great Dane; yet all men are part of the same human race, and all the varieties of dogs are dogs. Darwin came to the conclusion that variations occur in all animals and plants, and that the animal with a useful variation survives longer and therefore has more time to have more offspring. Often, some of these offspring will have the same variation, and the

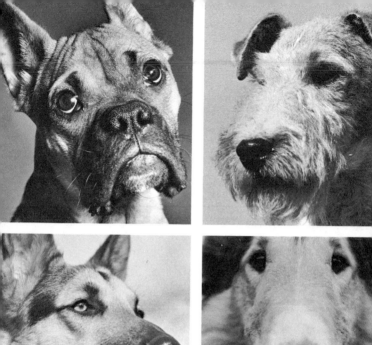

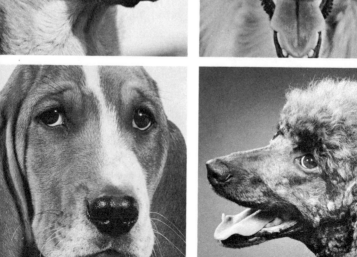

This is not evolution. Different breeds of dogs can be developed from a common ancestor, but all are still dogs.

variation may become increasingly prominent as generations roll by. Finally, generations later, the variation will be normal rather than being the exception. This is known as variation by natural selection.

The polar bear may be an example of natural selection. Of the various-colored bears that may once have inhabited the arctic, white bears are better protected from their enemies because they can't be seen against the snow. This could mean that white bears often lived longer than other colors of bears in the arctic and so were able to produce more offspring, until finally whiteness became standard.

But what has this to do with evolution? Well, everything! For it is not

claimed that one animal evolves suddenly into another—a reptile suddenly hatching into a bird, for example—but this is a process, says the evolutionist, that takes place over millions of years by very minute changes, generation after generation.

From observing variations that had become standard, Darwin came to the conclusion that all life began from some simple form. He reasoned that this simple form reproduced with slight variations that eventually became permanent. There were slight additional changes in later generations until finally the simple form of life, after a long process of constant mutations, and after hundreds of millions of years, became man.

The creationist of course does not
believe this. He believes that God
created man separately, and that man
did not evolve from a simple form
after ages of changes. The creationist
believes that although there are variations among dogs, there are no variations beyond dogness. The Great Dane
will not become, after millions of years,
anything but a dog.

The reasons for this belief of the
creationist are essentially two: The
laws of genetics as we know them do
not include this possibility; and the
fossils do not confirm that this has
happened in the past.

What Do the Chromosomes Say About Evolution?

The evolutionist says that the genes in the chromosomes of the early forms of life changed dramatically as the eons rolled along, building up additional codes that caused variations in the cells they controlled. These variations were so radical that ultimately the first single cell became a complex modern organism such as man.

Well, it is hard to disprove such a theory. All we can say is that in all the cases ever observed by anyone, this has not happened. Fifty years of fruit-fly experiments, equivalent to 1000 human generations, give no different reading. The Pekinese is still a dog and never develops into some-

thing else. Whether, given millions of
years, some unknown law of heredity
would be revealed, we do not know.
Unless this happened, the creationist
sees no way to save the case for
evolution.

What Do the Fossils Prove?

Why does the evolutionist believe
that the bear's ancestors (and the
ancestors of all mammals, including
man, and of all birds) were reptiles?

These days he usually begins his
proof with the fossil record. (Thirty
years ago he probably would have
begun with the argument that "ontogeny
recapitulates phylogeny"—that is, that
there are supposed similarities between,
for instance, the adult reptile and the
mammal embryo, and that these are
evidences for evolution. However,
present day evolutionists have abandoned this argument.)

So what does the fossil record
show? It seems to show that in the
earliest layers of the earth there were

smaller forms of life than those living in later layers.

Does the fossil record show that the ancestor of man is a reptile? No, it doesn't. Does it show that God created reptiles and bears as distinct creations? No, it doesn't show that either.

Why then does the evolutionist put so much value on the fossil evidence? How does he use it to support his views?

It is mostly a matter of logic. The early, smaller fossils preceded the later, larger ones, and so it is only reasonable, he says, to believe that the one came from the other. He cannot prove it, but it satisfies him.

The creationist, however, is far from satisfied with trying to settle the

The lower jaw of the Perry mastodon, discovered in an ancient swamp by excavators in October 1963, at Glen Ellyn, Illinois. Sixty percent of the bones were recovered, including this jaw, the skull and both tusks. The age is estimated at 11,000 years. Mastodons became extinct 8,000 years ago. These animals were similar to present day elephants (except in size!) but were not ancestral to them.

matter by evolutionary logic. For the evolutionist bases his argument on a presupposition that God didn't separately create the later forms of life. But this is exactly what the creationist thinks happened. (More accurately, *many* creationists think this. Other creationists doubt the validity of the fossil record altogether, and believe that all these kinds of life, both small and large, were created *simultaneously*.)

The creationist goes much further than objecting to the presupposition on which the evolutionist decides the matter. The creationist points out that the various kinds of animals appear suddenly without fossil links to connect them with earlier, sometimes smaller, forms.

26   The horse is a good example of this, for it is used as a standard argument by the evolutionist to show how evolution works. The facts, to which all evolutionists and most creationists can agree, are that the horse of 60,000,000 years ago was smaller and 4-toed as compared with today's 1-toed species. But as to the interpretation of these facts, the evolutionist sees in these changes not only the outworking of natural selection, but also proof that if we could only find the earlier fossils, they would show a continual, further gradation downward into some entirely different, dog-like or racoon-like animal. The only trouble is, the fossil record ends exactly where it does, with the 4-toed horse. And why does the

record stop there? Probably because that is where the horse began, for that is when God created it.

Does this horse sequence "prove" evolution? Can it not just as well "prove" creation? All available *evidence* points to a *sudden beginning* of the horse, small and 4-toed, containing genetic potential for differentiation into a 1-toed horse; also genetic potential for differences in sizes such as we have today, for instance, between the little Shetland pony and the huge Clydesdale draft horse.

Why do we not find, in the rich masses of fossils now available, a long series of fossils in known time-order, gradually becoming a horse? And since we do not find this series, is it because it didn't happen that way?

The evolutionist takes note of this and is much puzzled by the problem of missing links, but assumes that someday the gaps will be filled with the millions of links now missing.

But there is a further problem in the fossil record. Every major group (phylum) except perhaps the vertebrates is represented in the *lowest* fossil-bearing layers of the Cambrian, 600,000,000 years ago, with no evidence at all that one developed from the other. These facts are of course fully known and recognized by any competent evolutionist, but are laid aside with the hope that someday the puzzle will be explained.

But are there *no* links between the various major groups of animals in the fossil record, between the reptiles and the birds, for instance? Only a few possibilities have been discovered thus far in the fossil record. But with several millions of different kinds of fossil plants and animals known, it is only reasonable to expect that *millions* of links would have been found by now. There should be an infinite gradation from one kind of animal into another, but such is not the case.

30   Let us look at a creature claimed by the evolutionist to be one of these links: the Archaeornis. The evolutionist believes this "half bird, half beast" to be a link between the reptiles and the birds. It looks a bit like both (see illustration).

But the creationist sees no reason to think that it is. In the first place, if this were a link, would there not be many, many more links, showing a gradual development of bird-like structures and a gradual dropping away of the reptile-like features? (Or visa-versa —whether the Archaeornis was going up or down the supposed evolutionary ladder is indeterminable unless further links are located and dated.) But paleontologists have not discovered

The Archaeornis, from the Upper Jurassic, 180,000,000 years ago.

As all buildings use similar construction units, so also the Creator has used the cell and its fantastically complex components as the basic unit of all living material.

these other elements in the supposed chain. So the creationist's conclusion is that the further evidence probably doesn't exist, and that the Archaeornis is not evidence for evolution.

But why the similarities to reptile and bird in the same animal? Does not this *seem* to prove the evolutionist's hypothesis? No, replies the creationist, not necessarily, and for this reason: Was God as Creator required to make every kind of animal different from all others? Could He not use a basic pattern and then make some variations from it? To use an inadequate present-day analogy, if a carpenter builds a cottage and a mansion, is it illogical for him to build medium-income housing too, using basic rooms in all? Let

Cave drawings from 15,000 to 30,000 years ago. Do these prove evolution? No more than the present day American Indians do. Throughout history there have been cave-dwellers side by side with agriculturally-oriented peoples living in their tents, houses and other shelters.

Black Bull (detail of a cave painting).
c 15,000-10,000 B.C. Lascaux (Dordogue), France.

34   God be God and if He has occasionally created a creature that has features of two different groups, this only indicates to the creationist that God, with His infinite varieties, created it that way. But to the evolutionist, Archaeornis is one of the few links he has found of the millions needed to support his theory.

What About Good
Old Neanderthal?

Now we turn to the interesting questions about fossil man and cave drawings. How old are these and where do they fit into the creationist's scheme of things?

As to the age of man, the creationist and the evolutionist have the

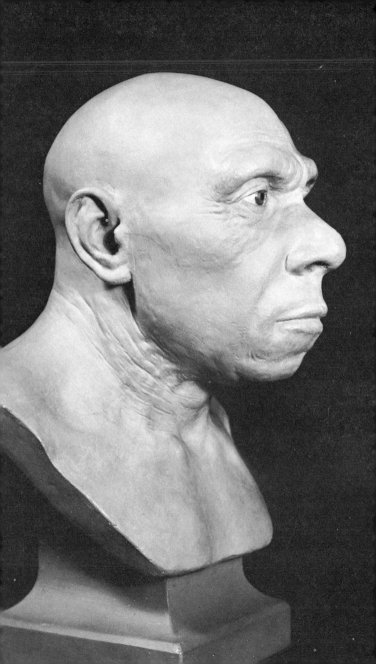

Neanderthal man.

37

same data, with estimates ranging up
to 1,750,000 years if some recent South
African finds are actually those of man
and not of an ape. (There is no agree-
ment yet by anthropologists on this
interesting point.) So from the creationist viewpoint at this time, the picture is this: All fossil men and women
are descendants of Adam and Eve, who
were created directly by God, so Adam
and Eve are older than the earliest
human fossils.

The Bible gives no evidence upon
which we can draw to determine the
time of Adam's creation. Genealogi-
cal tables of the Bible, in the Hebrew
usage, list only representative ancestors
and are not a complete listing. So the
Bible permits millions of years as

easily as thousands, and is not helpful in deciding this question as to when Adam was created.

And what of the cave men, the picture painters of ancient Europe? Do they prove evolution? No, no more than the American Indian cliff-dwellers of Arizona. Today, and in every age, some have lived in caves. This does not make them any less human, and adds no weight to the evolutionist's claim that modern man has evolved from these earlier men.

But is it not true that the Heidelberg man, the Neanderthal, etc. are stooped and ape-like in appearance, and therefore are obviously in the line of ascent from molecule to man? No, no more than differences in facial feature and body structure of modern man prove this. The tall Watusi African, the pigmy, the flat-nosed Asiatic, the Negro with his distinctive features—all are variations within the human family. So also ancient men probably varied from each other and from us today.

But this is not evidence for evolution
any more than is the 4-toed horse.
Man is still man.

(By the way, recently a "new look"
has been given to some of the ancient
human fossils, and they are being pic-
tured as less stooped and "ape-like"
than the earlier reconstruction efforts,
influenced as they no doubt were by
the assumption that early man would
be ape-like in appearance.)

Did Life Evolve from
Inorganic Matter?

Can life develop from non-living
material? If not, evolution gets off to
a shaky start. It was once thought that
flies in manure piles were examples of
spontaneous generation. Then came
Louis Pasteur who showed that the flies
came from eggs that had been laid there
by other flies. The idea of spontaneous
generation had to be abandoned. However, in recent years the theoretical
possibility of developing lifelike (though
not necessarily living) molecules has

become an apparent possibility. Although the idea that a rock might become an animal is manifestly absurd, it doesn't seem so preposterous when the rock is reduced in thought to primordial ooze.

Professor A.I. Oparin, author of *The Origin of Life* (New York: Mac-Millan Co., 1938), believed that simple, organic, lifelike compounds such as hydro-carbons might arise spontaneously under careful laboratory conditions.

Building upon Oparin's work, S.L. Miller of the College of Physicians and Surgeons, Columbia University, passed an electric spark through an atmosphere of gases such as the primitive atmosphere on earth would need to be composed of, if spontaneous generation could succeed. The apparent result was the formation of amino acids under these laboratory conditions.

Then, according to the theory of evolution, these tiny molecules, formed perhaps by an electric charge, found each other, clumped together, and

Dr. Stanley Miller, whose experiment of passing a current through gases yielded several organic molecules. Formation of life, or imitation of life-like molecules in a test tube now seems a likely possibility. To get the molecules to reproduce is quite another matter.

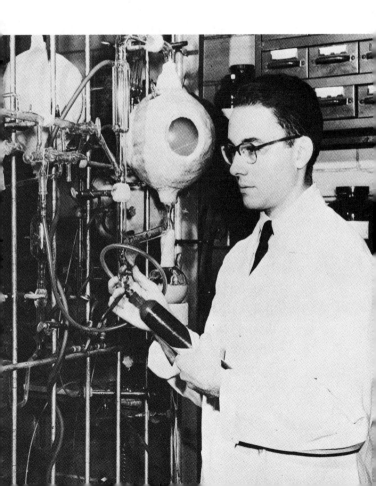

interacted to form huge protein molecules large enough to bear life.

To the creationist this is interesting speculation, but is too far removed from probability to render it valuable. *If* by accident and chance the complex proteins were formed is a big *if*.

But some evolutionists suggest that given enough time, *anything* can happen by chance. Dr. Harlow Shapley of Harvard University is quoted in *Science Newsletter* (July 3, 1965) as saying, "Life occurs automatically whenever the conditions are right. It will not only emerge but persist and evolve."

Yet men of equal ability doubt this. For instance, Malcom Dixon and E.C. Webb in their learned work on enzymes *(Enzymes,* second edition, New York: Academic Press, Inc. 1964, page 665) make this remark: "To say airily, as some do, that whenever conditions are suitable for life to exist, life will inevitably emerge, is to betray a complete ignorance of the problems involved."

Many of the scientists present at the symposium on the origin of life held at Moscow in August, 1957, felt that Oparin's idea that lifelike molecules could rise spontaneously was incredible. They could not and did not believe that large enough molecules of the right kinds of proteins could arise spontaneously to become the basis of organic life. Dr. Erwin Chartaff of Columbia University remarks, "Our time is probably the first in which mythology has penetrated to the molecular level!" (Erwin Chartaff, "Nucleic Acids As Carriers of Biological Information," *The Origin of Life on the Earth,* pages 298-99)

A "simple" cell, the basic structure of all life, is far from simple. One of its machines is the DNA molecule; each DNA molecule contains 4 billion items of information! Another of its mechanisms, for which evolution can give no plausible explanation, is the complex mitotic apparatus causing division and duplication of the cell.

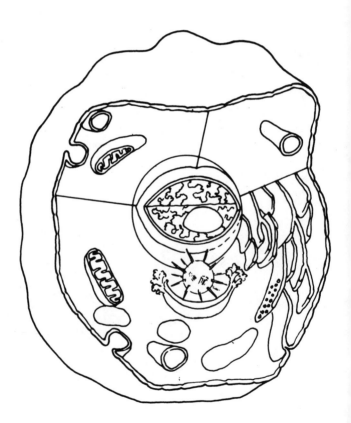

The next step in the theory is that these large molecules somehow inter- acted to form "simple" cells. But see the accompanying illustration to ob- serve the complexity of the most simple! Millions of protein molecules would have had to "spontaneously generate" simultaneously, not here and there around the world but in the same pond and at the same time. And then by strict accident and chance they would begin to "count off" and form themselves into various parts of the protozoa or other complex single- celled units. Notice carefully the accompanying diagram of DNA, just one of the amazing "machines" in every cell.

This drawing attempts to show some details of how the DNA in the chromosomes controls every aspect of body formation, and presumably of temperament, personality and all other phases of heredity. A notched tape moves across the base, indicating which of the far more than 100,000 protein molecules are to be formed. How the tape knows when to stop is still unknown. This incredibly sophisticated "computerized" factory seems unlikely to be a product of a succession of mutations.

The protein factory in every cell

Newly manufactured protein strand

Transfer-RNA deciphers the ticker-tape and produces the new strand above

Coded ticker-tape

Ribosome

A model of a double-helix molecule of DNA. Did this gradually evolve, or did God create it? That is the basic question this book is trying to bring into focus.

Julian Huxley, born in 1887, is a British biologist and naturalist who has been the most ardent modern exponent of Darwinianism.

48

Does all this seem incredible? Yes, it does! But given enough eons of time, might not the impossible become possible? T.H. Huxley, a friend of Charles Darwin and grandfather of today's famous evolutionist Sir Julian Huxley, puts in stark relief the claim that *anything* can *eventually* happen by chance, a proposition the evolutionist can scarcely do without.

He declared that if a band of monkeys sat at typewriters and were given enough time—millions of years— it would be inevitable that at some time during this long period of time they would type the *Encyclopedia Brittanica* word for word and in exact order. Much of evolution requires this same degree of faith. Yet, until a

A major presupposition of evolution is that, given enough time, anything can happen by chance. The creationist doubts this, noting that chance can tear down as well as build up.

better theory is proposed, evolution
seems to many scientists to be too neat
a solution to many problems to be set
aside lightly. Especially since the
alternative—creation by God—is felt
somehow to be too "easy" a solution,
requiring too much faith.

That life generated spontaneously
is like saying that given enough time, a
house could build itself—that by chance
through millions of years, occasional
hurricanes would cause every board
and nail of a house to fit perfectly into
place, the plumbing to be installed,
the carpets to be carefully laid on the
floors. There are, however, two problems apart from the question of enough
time: First, will the lumber last, or
will it be ravaged by time, or knocked

52   apart again by one of the hurricanes?
Secondly, will chance also produce
the needed lumber mills, nail factories
and carpet looms? Let us look for a
possible method: a hunk of metal from
a meteor lying in some field was picked
up by a cyclone and worn flat to make
a saw blade, then made jagged at the
edges and transported to where other
machinery, including electric motors
and IBM computer equipment, was
being assembled, all by chance and
time.

This is an explanation of how a
house might build itself. But it doesn't
prove that it happened.

So also the explanation of molecular formation by Oparin and others
does not prove that it happened that

way. The self-built house probably involves fewer improbabilities than the development of the first molecule, or the first cell containing the fantastic, incredible DNA apparatus and all the other "plumbing and carpets"—enzymes, mitotic apparatus, etc., etc.

No, a theory of how something *might have* happened may have little relationship to what *did* actually happen. And as to the theory that anything is possible by chance, given enough time: zero possibility multiplied by infinity still yields zero.

The acceptance of this basic, cardinal presupposition of many evolutionists, that life generated spontaneously, must be questioned by thoughtful high school students even though

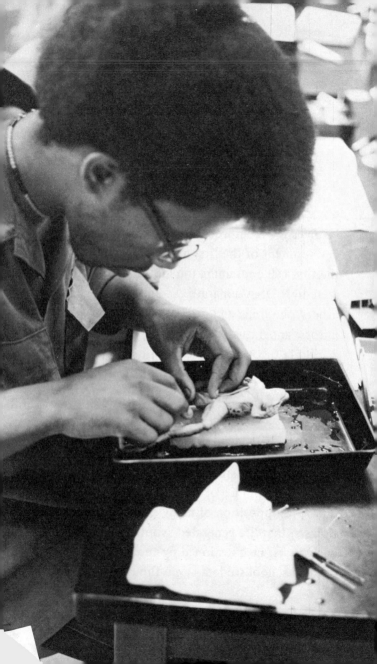

it be presented to them by good
teachers and good textbooks. There
comes a time when a person must think
for himself.

The Vestigial Organs

A further evidence of evolution,
to the evolutionist, are the so-called
vestigial organs. For instance the appendix, which, according to the evolutionist,
was used by man's ancestors who ate
much cellulose. Since cellulose would
require a much larger digestive organ
than modern man's stomach, the
appendix is supposed to have been a
large addition to the bowel system, now
no longer needed. But is this suggested
explanation a proof? No, merely a
theory that perhaps proves too much:
what shall we say of the vestigial breasts
and nipples possessed by every man
and other male mammal? Shall we
say that man once suckled his babies?

UNnatural Selection?

One of the beliefs of the evolutionist most difficult to accept is his assertion that tiny random mutations,
during millions of years, become complex new organs such as the eye and
ear. These incomplete changes would
often be detrimental to the animal
during millions of years until the final
organ was completed. Why then would
they be selected? Why would these
apparently pointless or unvaluable changes
be preserved by natural selection?

The evolutionist explains that each
tiny mutation which will produce prog-
ress is somehow beneficial, or at least
not lethal, and waits until another
mutation appears with which it can
cooperate. This is difficult to accept.

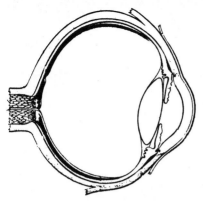

It would appear that here is a situation where an explanation does not really explain. It may be a necessity to help the theory more than it is a fact.

As to the incredibly complex eye, George L. Walls, in his book *The Vertebrate Eye,* quotes Froriep as saying, "It appears fully formed as though sprung from the brow of Zeus." If so, this is amazing—so amazing that the creationist feels that his case is enormously strengthened. For if the eye didn't come by slow mutations, (and no evolutionist is suggesting that it came all at once as a major mutation), then creation seems to be the logical answer.

A perhaps even greater difficulty for the evolutionist are the male and female copulatory organs of mammals. For until these organs are complete, they are useless. And meanwhile, if the organs are not available for use, that kind of animal is doomed to quick extinction because it is without posterity.

The evolutionist may suggest possible transition organs during the eons until the present copulatory organs became functional, but once again there is no evidence that this was the case, or reason for incomplete copulatory organs to be selected by nature. Without doubt the evidence favors the creationist in this vast area of essential organs. Again let it be said that half-formed organs would usually be in the way rather than beneficial, and would be passed over by natural selection, rather than being chosen. And how could the copulatory system of the mammal be valuable until complete? A half-formed male organ could not produce and inject sperm into the female, nor could a half-formed egg production system of the female be of any value. Why then would it be chosen? The better answer would seem to be that these organs were not formed by natural selection, but by creation along with the entire species.

24-Hour Days of Creation?

The question often rises among creationists as to the length of the "days" of creation mentioned in the Bible (Genesis 1). Were these 24-hour days? The answer lies in the fact that the Hebrew word translated "day" in the first chapter of Genesis can equally well be translated "period of time." How long is a "period of time"? The word is completely indefinite. It might refer to 24 hours and it might be millions of years. Apparently each day in Genesis was of millions of year's duration, if the normal system of dating fossils is accepted. In fact, snails appear in the fossil record 450,000,000 years ago! Man is perhaps up to a million years old! So we are talking about days 100,000,000 years long!

The "Family Tree of Man" according to the evolutionist.
But to detail an idea is not to prove it. The factual evidence is largely missing.

Another possibility urged by some creationists is that the days were 24 hours long, and all creation was finished in a 7-day week. To accept this idea requires believing that the fossil layers are meaningless; that they were planted by God at the time of creation rather than being laid down by geological action; or that the layers were all somehow formed in the year of Noah's flood.

To me it appears that God's special creative acts occurred many times during six long geological periods, capped by the creation of Adam and Eve perhaps a million or more years ago. This idea seems to do justice both to the Bible and to what geologists and anthropologists currently believe. If they change their dates up or down, it will make no difference to this belief, unless to move Adam's age forward or backwards.

"The Phylogeny of the Primates." Here again, the visual presentation helps us understand the theory, but the question is, did it happen that way? Other theories are equally credible and may be as easily assumed. Alert students who are not bound to biological traditions should be fully informed of alternative possibilities and be ready to examine them carefully.

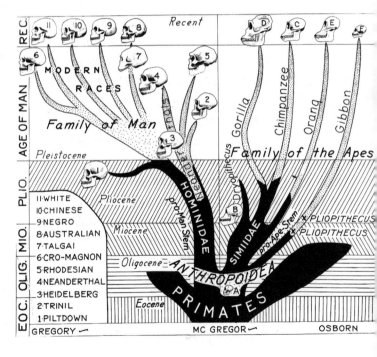

Theistic Evolution?

And now what about theistic evolution: the belief that God used evolutionary processes such as natural selection to bring a man's body into being, and then at some point God placed a spirit into that man-like body, so that it became a true man, Adam?

Well, if there is insufficient evidence for plain evolution, then there is also insufficient evidence for theistic evolution. But if you believe in evolution, can you still accept the Bible, or must you throw away your faith?

No, don't throw away your faith! The Bible account can be read to harmonize with current science, if you insist! To me this seems unwise, unnecessary, and wrong, but here is

the formula: Just assume that when I,
as a creationist, read the first chapter
of Genesis, I am reading into it something that isn't there. For I assume
that it says that the creation of man
was instantaneous. But when the Bible
says, "God created man in His own
image," perhaps this doesn't say or
mean "instantaneously," but means
instead that "God created man (by a
long process of evolution) in His own
image." You can argue that since the
Bible is not quite clear on this point,
it is not unBiblical to believe either
way you like. Among British evangeli-
cals this view is fairly common—that
God used evolution to form man. But
it is not my own view at all, as you will
know by now!

66   Remember, too, that the Bible's principal purpose is to reveal to all mankind the kindness and power of God to forgive our sins under the conditions the Bible sets forth. There is no controversy about this. Whatever you decide about evolution has no relationship to this far-reaching, utterly basic fact of sin and salvation.

The theory of evolution, although widely accepted, is based on many presuppositions. (One current, major textbook on evolution labels as assumptions twelve unprovable factors that are required as articles of faith to make the theory work.) So the theory is very far from proved, but is a convenient explanation for those who find it difficult to believe in instantaneous creation.

However, the theory of evolution is difficult to accept because it has so little evidence. The fossil record does not seem to correlate well with the theory because the fact is that each major kind of plant and animal appears suddenly without intermediate forms connecting it to earlier forms. To the

creationist this means that God created
these new forms from time to time
without connection to previous forms.
In each case God used the same cellu-
lar structure as part of His master plan,
just as a builder uses lumber, windows
and roofs for all sizes and styles of
houses.

The theory of evolution also seems
totally inadequate in solving the problem caused by another of its assumptions—that organs of the body evolved
gradually through tiny mutations,
selected by survival of the fittest. For
these half-formed organs would often
be detrimental, and would not be
selected for survival. An eye, for
instance, would hardly evolve slowly
by chance mutations through millions
of years. It requires a master archi-
tect. Male and female reproductive
systems are another example.

Furthermore, the theory is entirely
unreasonable in its assumption that
such amazing units as cells, packed
with chromosomes and other incredibly

sophisticated machines like DNA,
would develop by the chance organi-
zation of molecules, in turn formed by
chance from inorganic material.

Conclusion

1. There is no hard evidence for evolution in the fossil records.

2. There is no sound theoretical basis
for "upward" development, since the
science of genetics as we know it does
not permit variations apart from what
is inherent in the original genes.

3. There is no imaginable way for
chromosomes, genes, enzymes, DNA,
etc., to have developed by chance and
natural selection.

4. There is no evidence that "nature"
has creative goals towards which it
works for millions of years. This in-
vests the blind forces of nature with
foresight and personality. This concept
of nature sounds like another name
for God.

5. There is no way for complex organs to arise by minute and progressive mutations; natural selection would eliminate these useless pre-organs, instead of encouraging them.

6. There is no proof for the existence in nature of such a process as natural selection except for minor variations of size, color, facial feature, etc.